CHOCOLATE
CAKES & DECORATIONS

JOANNA FARROW
CONSULTANT · LINDSAY JOHN BRADSHAW

MEREHURST

I dedicate this book to my parents,
for all their help and support.

≈

Published in 1992 by Merehurst Limited, Ferry House,
51-57 Lacy Road, Putney, London SW15 1PR

Managing Editor Katie Swallow
Edited by Jenni Fleetwood
Designed by Peter Bridgewater
Photography by James Duncan
Colour Separation by Fotographics Ltd, UK - Hong Kong
Printed by Wing King Tong Ltd, Hong Kong

NOTES ON USING THE RECIPES

For all recipes, quantities are given in metric, Imperial and cup measurements. Follow one set of measures only as they are not interchangeable. Standard 5ml teaspoons (tsp) and 15ml tablespoons (tbsp) are used. Australian readers, whose tablespoons measure 20ml, should adjust quantities accordingly.
All spoon measures are assumed to be level unless otherwise stated.
Ovens should be pre–heated to specified temperatures.
Microwave oven timings are based on a 650 watt output.
Eggs are a standard size 3 unless otherwise stated.
Where chocolate squares are listed in ingredients lists, this applies to American readers.

CONTENTS

INTRODUCTION

*M*ost people enthuse at the mere mention of chocolate, so the appearance of mouthwatering chocolate cakes, whether simple or elaborate, is sure to meet with approval and requests for more.

This book gives an insight into the scope that chocolate cookery offers and is a companion volume to Simple Cakes: Icings & Frostings in the Sugarcraft Skills Series. It shows how, with a developing range of skills, both novices and experienced cooks can create attractive and delicious chocolate cakes. All the ingredients used are readily available and, with a few exceptions, most of the equipment is already to be found in most kitchens.

The opening chapters give recipes for basic cakes as well as a varied selection of icings, pastes and fillings. There is also a chapter on basic techniques, including melting, dipping, colouring, moulding and shaping chocolate for both novel and traditional decorations. This is followed by a collection of stunning chocolate cakes from teatime treats to elaborate celebration centrepieces. There is a novelty clown, a Christmas wreath, a chocolate parcel – even an impressive three–tier wedding cake. Each chapter includes step–by–step photographs to show how easy it can be to create highly professional results.

All the basic cakes can be made in advance and stored in the freezer; Madeira cakes improve if made a day or two in advance. Genoese sponges and roulades are best eaten within 48 hours.

The ideas and techniques covered by this book are easy to learn and can be adapted to suit personal tastes. Whether you favour traditional or novelty cakes, there is great satisfaction to be found in inventing original designs to share with family and friends.

ALL ABOUT CHOCOLATE

Chocolate is derived from the cacao tree, which thrives in tropical countries, particularly equatorial South America. The fruits of the tree, cacao pods, are about the size of a small melon. The immature greenish yellow fruits slowly turn red as they ripen, ready for harvesting twice yearly. Once harvested, each pod is split open to reveal 30 or 40 oval beans enclosed in a white fruit pulp. The beans are extracted and left to ferment for several days. During fermentation they turn dark brown and develop their chocolaty flavour, ready to be transformed into chocolate. After roasting and shelling the beans are pressed. From this pressing chocolate liquor and cocoa butter are produced. Some of the chocolate liquor is pressed to form bitter chocolate but the majority of it is processed further, either by being dried and made into cocoa powder or by being combined with cocoa butter and other ingredients to form chocolate in its most familiar form.

Most of the chocolate we buy is made from a combination of chocolate liquor, cocoa butter, sugar and milk, with the exception of white chocolate, which contains no chocolate liquor and is very sweet and waxy. Milk (German sweet) chocolate has a higher percentage of milk added than plain (semisweet) chocolate.

During processing, chocolate is blended and stirred to give it its characteristic smooth, creamy texture. It is the time taken in this important process, together with the quality of the bean and percentage of cocoa solids used in the recipe that determines the quality of the chocolate. In the final stage of the process the chocolate is moulded and wrapped.

TYPES OF CHOCOLATE

❖

Several types of chocolate are suitable for baking. Top of the range is *couverture*, the purest form of chocolate. Made from cocoa liquor, sugar and cocoa butter, it gives a smooth glossy result and has a good flavour. Because it contains a complex mixture of fats with different melting and setting points however, couverture must be 'tempered' before use. This means heating and cooling the chocolate several times to precise temperatures, a process that is discussed in greater depth on page 62. When tempering is complete, *couverture* can be used like any other chocolate. It is possible to buy tempered chocolate in block form from cake decorating shops.

Bakers' (compound) chocolate varies from *couverture* in that most of the cocoa butter has been removed and replaced with a vegetable fat. This eliminates the need for tempering, making it far more suitable for anyone new to chocolate work. The best quality has a cocoa solid quantity of at least 47 percent and is designed for melting and cooking. Look out for it at cake decorating shops and supermarkets.

The most widely available chocolate is the type sold as confectionery, stocked on supermarket shelves, confectionery counters and in sweet (candy) shops as bars, buttons or drops. These are perfectly acceptable for chocolate cooking but it should be remembered that milk (German sweet) chocolate and white chocolate have a less intense flavour than plain (semisweet) chocolate.

CHOCOLATE-FLAVOURED CAKE COVERINGS These are also available in supermarkets, but should not be confused with pure chocolate. Chocolate–flavoured cake coverings have a high proportion of vegetable oil, combined with sugar, cocoa (unsweetened cocoa powder), milk powder and flavourings. They are inferior in both flavour and texture.

CHOCOLATE CHIPS (bits) are used for decorating novelty cakes, adding to cake mixtures and easy melting. Buttons are used in much the same way, while chocolate vermicelli (sprinkles) are frequently used on small cakes and to coat truffles, see page 31.

COCOA (unsweetened cocoa powder) This has a high starch content. When used in baking, it should replace some of the measured flour.

DRINKING CHOCOLATE (sweetened cocoa powder) Ready sweetened, this has a mild flavour and is best kept for drinks or for dusting over cakes.

CAROB derives from the pods of the carob tree, which is no relation to the cacao. Available in powder and block form, it is used as a chocolate substitute for those allergic to chocolate.

WORKING WITH CHOCOLATE

Chocolate is an exciting ingredient, but can be somewhat temperamental and frustrating to deal with, particularly for beginners. Careful melting, see page 16, is crucial as overheating results in a disappointing discoloration that unfortunately appears only once the chocolate has set. The smallest droplet of water coming into contact with the melted chocolate can also make it thicken and spoil.

STORING CHOCOLATE

In a dry place and with optimum temperature conditions (about 20°C/68 °F) chocolate can be stored successfully for up to a year. If the temperature is too hot the chocolate will develop a greyish white bloom, the result of the fat content coming to the surface. Although this will not spoil the flavour – and the chocolate can still be melted for adding to cakes and icings – it is preferable to use fresh chocolate for decorative work.

Chocolate should not be stored in the refrigerator and should only be chilled in the refrigerator for a short while to speed setting as prolonged chilling could also lead to discoloration. Freezing should also be avoided for more than a minute or two as condensation may occur.

*M*ost of the equipment required for chocolate work will be found in the average kitchen. These items are listed alphabetically below, together with some more specialized equipment which is available from cake decorating shops or good kitchenware stores.

BISCUIT (COOKIE) AND PASTRY CUTTERS These come in numerous shapes and sizes, including stars, hearts, trees, flowers, crescents and letters. Useful for shaping small chocolate biscuits or cutouts.

CAKE DECORATING SCRAPERS Usually made in plastic, these come with a variety of decorative edges from simple serrating to more elaborate designs. They can be used to texture the surface of a chocolate-covered cake or to create a pattern on a cake covered in buttercream.

CHOCOLATE MOULDS These come in traditional Easter egg shapes or as novelty items, including teddies, mice, snowmen and butterflies.

COCKTAIL STICKS (toothpicks) Wooden sticks are invaluable for adding paste food colouring and as a handling tool in delicate chocolate work.

DIPPING FORK A narrow-pronged fork used for dipping fruits, nuts and truffles in chocolate. A pickle fork kept specifically for chocolate work or an ordinary fork with narrow prongs may be used instead.

DOUBLE SAUCEPAN (double boiler) A saucepan which incorporates an inner pan or bowl, designed to allow water to be heated in the base. The contents of the upper section cook without the application of direct heat. Used primarily for melting chocolate and in sauce making. A double saucepan can be improvised by placing a closely fitting heatproof bowl over a small pan. There should be no gap between pan and bowl to allow steam to escape.

GREASEPROOF PAPER (parchment) Used for lining tins (pans) and making templates. Good quality parchment is used for making piping bags, see page 17.

HEAVY-BOTTOMED SAUCEPAN This is recommended for those occasions when it is desirable to melt chocolate over direct heat, for instance when mixed with butter and syrup for a sauce. The heavy base reduces the risk of the chocolate sauce catching.

PAINTBRUSHES Set aside several new paint brushes specifically for painting leaves with chocolate or for attaching decorations to cakes.

PALETTE KNIFE Useful for spreading chocolate icings and creams and for lifting delicate chocolate decorations off paper. It is worth buying at least two sizes.

PAPER PIPING BAGS These can be bought for convenience or made at home. See page 17 for step-by-step instructions.

PAPER SWEET CASES (candy cups) These come in a good variety of colours for serving chocolate truffles and other sweets. Plain ones are used as chocolate cases.

PIPING TUBES (tips) Of the huge variety stocked in cake decorating shops, only two, a writing tube and a star tube are necessary for most simple chocolate decorations.

TURNTABLE A worthwhile purchase for large scale cake decorating as it allows the cake to be readily rotated.

WAX PAPER This is easier to peel away from runouts and cutouts than greaseproof paper (parchment).

LINING TINS (PANS)

Correct lining of tins not only prevents cake mixture from sticking; it also helps to ensure a well shaped cake. Brush tins with melted vegetable fat (shortening), lard or oil, line with greaseproof paper (parchment), then lightly grease paper.

SWISS ROLL TIN (jelly roll pan) Place tin on a piece of greaseproof paper (parchment) and draw around base. Cut around shape, leaving a 2.5cm (1 in) margin all round. Cut diagonally in from corners to marked lines. Brush tin with fat; press paper into tin so cut corners overlap. Grease paper.

SANDWICH TINS (pans) Brush with fat. Line bases only with circles of paper; grease paper.

HEART-SHAPED TIN (pan) Lay tin on paper; draw around base. Cut out shape. Line sides of tin as illustrated right for deep round and square cake tins, then press paper heart into base. Grease paper.

PUDDING BASINS AND OVENPROOF BOWLS Cut a circle of paper slightly larger than base of basin. Make 1cm (½ in) snips at intervals from edges towards centre. Brush basin with fat; press circle into base. Grease paper.

LOAF TIN (pan) Cut a strip of paper the length of tin base and long enough to cover base and long sides. Fit into greased tin. Line ends of tin separately; grease paper.

DEEP ROUND AND SQUARE TINS (pans) Cut a paper strip the circumference of tin and 2.5cm (1 in) deeper. Fold over one long edge; snip at intervals. Position strip in greased tin with snipped edge flat on base; cover with paper circle or square.

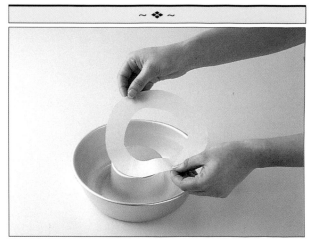

RING TIN (tube pan) Draw around base of tin on paper. Cut out shape; fold in half. Cut out circle slightly larger than centre of tin. Brush tin with fat and fit paper into base. Crease into place with pastry brush dipped in melted fat.

VICTORIA SANDWICH CAKE

*W*hile this light, soft–textured cake is designed to be simply sandwiched with jam or cream and dusted with icing (confectioners') sugar, it may be iced in more elaborate ways. The basic cake can be left plain or flavoured to complement the chosen icing or topping, see Flavourings right. The undecorated cake stores well for several days and may be frozen for up to 1 month. The quantities below are suitable for two 20cm (8 in) round layers. See chart for other sizes.

185g (6 oz) butter, softened
185g (6 oz/³/₄ cup) caster (superfine) sugar
3 eggs, lightly beaten
185g (6 oz/1¹/₂ cups) self–raising flour

● Preheat oven to 180°C (350°F/Gas 4). Grease and line cake tins (pans), following instructions on page 9.
● Beat butter and sugar together in a bowl, using either a wooden spoon or an electric mixer. When ready, mixture will be pale in colour and light and fluffy in consistency. It should drop easily from the spoon.
● Add beaten eggs, a little at a time, beating well between each addition. A tablespoon of the flour, added to mixture with eggs, will prevent curdling.
● Sift remaining flour into bowl and fold in using a large metal tablespoon until just combined. Do not overmix.
● Scrape mixture into prepared tins (pans) and level surfaces with the back of the spoon. Bake for 20–25 minutes or until top springs back when lightly pressed.
● Leave to cool slightly in tins (pans), then invert onto wire rack to cool completely. Remove lining paper.

FLAVOURINGS

The following flavour variations all go well with chocolate icings and coverings:

CHOCOLATE For each egg used, substitute 1 tbsp flour with 1 tbsp cocoa(unsweetened cocoa powder), sifting cocoa with flour.

CHOCOLATE CHIP For each egg used, add 30g (1 oz) chocolate chips (bits) to mixture.

MIXED NUTS For each egg used, add 30g (1 oz/¹/₄ cup) mixed nuts to mixture.

VICTORIA SANDWICH CAKE - QUANTITIES CHART

For a 2–egg mixture, reduce the quantity of butter to 125g (4 oz), the caster (superfine) sugar to 125g (4 oz/¹/₂ cup) and the flour to 125g (4 oz/1 cup). Double these quantities for a 4–egg mixture.

Number of eggs	Tin (pan) size	Cooking time @ 180°C (350°F/Gas 4)
2	two 18cm (7in) sandwich tins	20 minutes
	940ml (1¹/₂ pt) ring tin	25 minutes
3	two 20cm (8 in) sandwich tins	20–25 minutes
	28 x 18 x 4cm (11x7x1¹/₂ in) shallow baking tin	40 minutes
4	two 23cm (9 in) sandwich tins	25–30 minutes

QUICK MIX SPONGE

185g (6 oz) soft margarine
185g (6 oz/³/₄ cup) caster (superfine) sugar
3 eggs
185g (6oz/1¹/₂ cups) self–raising flour
1 tsp baking powder

Preheat oven to 160°C (325°F/Gas 3). Base line and grease two 20cm (8 in) round sandwich tins. Beat ingredients for 2–3 minutes with an electric mixer until light and fluffy. Spoon into tins; bake for 25–30 minutes until golden and firm.

GENOESE SPONGE

*M*ade by whisking sugar and eggs to an aerated foam, Genoese sponges are particularly light. The quantities below are suitable for two 18cm (7 in) round sandwich cakes. For two 20cm (8 in) round sandwich cakes, increase the sugar to 125g (4 oz/¹/₂ cup), the eggs to 4, the flour to 125g (4 oz/1 cup) and the melted butter to 60g (2 oz/¹/₄ cup).

3 eggs
90g (3 oz/¹/₃ cup) caster (superfine) sugar
90g (3 oz/³/₄ cup) plain (all–purpose) flour
45g (1¹/₂ oz/3 tbsp) butter, melted

● Preheat oven to 180°C (350°F/Gas 4). Base line and grease two cake tins (pans), see page 9.
● Combine eggs and sugar in a heatproof bowl. Set over hot but not boiling water and whisk as described right.

● Sift half the flour over the whisked mixture. Carefully fold in, using a metal tablespoon. Fold in half the melted butter, then fold in remaining flour and butter.
● Pour mixture into tins (pans), gently tilting tins so mixture spreads to corners. Bake for 15–20 minutes until golden and just firm to the touch. Cool slightly in tins, then invert onto a wire rack to cool completely. Remove lining paper.

FLAVOURINGS
CHOCOLATE Substitute 15g (¹/₂ oz/2 tbsp) flour with cocoa (unsweetened cocoa powder).
MOCHA As chocolate, adding 1 tbsp instant coffee powder dissolved in 2 tsp boiling water, with the butter.

GENOESE MIXTURE *Have ready sifted flour (with cocoa if using) and melted butter. Using an electric mixer, whisk egg and sugar mixture until pale and thick enough to hold the trail of a whisk, then remove bowl from pan.*

MADEIRA CAKE

*F*irm textured and easy to slice, Madeira cake is perfect for cutting into shapes for novelty cakes.

250g (8 oz) butter, softened
250g (8 oz/1 cup) caster (superfine) sugar
grated rind and juice of 1 lemon or orange
5 eggs, beaten
220g (7 oz/1¾ cups) self–raising flour
90g (3 oz/¾ cup) plain (all–purpose) flour

● Preheat oven to 160°C (325°F/Gas 3). Fully line and grease a 20cm (8 in) round cake tin (pan) or an 18cm (7 in) square cake tin, see page 9.

● In a warm bowl, cream butter and sugar with citrus rind, using either a wooden spoon or an electric mixer, until pale and fluffy.

● Gradually add eggs, beating well after each addition. A tablespoon of the flour, added with the eggs, will prevent curdling. Stir in juice.

● Sift flours together and gradually fold in, using a large metal tablespoon. Scrape mixture into tin (pan). Smooth surface. Bake for 1½ hours until firm to the touch. A skewer inserted in the centre of the cake should come out clean. Cool slightly in the tin, then invert on a wire rack to cool completely. Remove lining paper.

FLAVOURINGS

CHOCOLATE CHIP Add 60g (2 oz/⅓ cup) chocolate chips (bits) with citrus juice.

DOUBLE CHOCOLATE Omit citrus rind and juice and substitute 30g (1 oz/¼ cup) plain (all–purpose) flour with 30g (1 oz/¼ cup) cocoa (unsweetened cocoa powder). Add 60g (2 oz/⅓ cup) chocolate chips (bits).

CHOCOLATE ROULADE

5 eggs, separated
185g (6 oz/¾ cup) caster (superfine) sugar
185g (6 oz/6 squares) white or plain (semisweet) chocolate
caster (superfine) sugar for dusting

● Preheat oven to 180°C (350°F/Gas 4). Line and grease 33 x 23cm (13 x 9 in) Swiss roll tin (jelly roll pan), see page 9. Beat egg yolks with 155g (5 oz/⅔ cup) of the sugar until pale and thick. Melt chocolate, then stir it in. Add egg whites with remaining sugar, following instructions below. Transfer mixture to tin. Bake for 20 minutes. Cover with a dampened tea towel; cool. Invert onto greaseproof paper (parchment) dusted with caster sugar.

Whisk egg whites in a clean, greasefree bowl until stiff. Gradually beat in remaining caster (superfine) sugar. Using a large metal tablespoon, carefully fold into white or dark chocolate mixture. Do not beat or mixture will deflate.

CHOCOLATE MOUSSE CAKE

*A*s the name suggests, Chocolate Mousse cake is very moist, rich and mousse–like in texture. Use plain (semisweet) chocolate, milk (German sweet) or white chocolate – all give good results. After baking the cake will sink slightly in the tin (pan). This is perfectly normal and will not affect the flavour or texture. Once made, the cake can be decorated quite simply with soured or whipped cream and finished with chocolate curls or caraque, see page 18. For a more elaborate finish, try the Christmas wreath on page 46.

*185g (6 oz/6 squares) plain
(semisweet) chocolate
60g (2 oz) butter
6 eggs, separated
90g (3 oz/$^1/_3$ cup) caster (superfine) sugar
125g (4 oz/ 1 cup) ground almonds*

● Preheat oven to 180°C (350°F/ Gas 4). Base line and grease a 20cm (8 in) round cake tin (pan), see page 9. Melt the chocolate with the butter in a bowl set over hot water.
● Using an electric mixer, whisk the egg yolks in a bowl with half the sugar until thick and pale. Whisk in the melted chocolate mixture.
● Thoroughly clean and dry the whisks, then beat the egg whites in a clean greasefree bowl until stiff. Add the remaining sugar, whisking well after each addition, and fold in the ground almonds, following detailed instructions right.
● Using a large metal tablespoon, carefully fold the chocolate mixture into the whites until just incorporated.

● Scrape the mixture into the tin (pan) and bake for 40 minutes until the cake has a firm crust. Leave to cool in the tin. Loosen edges of cake with a knife before inverting onto a wire rack or plate. Remove lining paper.

EXPERT ADVICE

≈

Chocolate Mousse Cake should be baked as soon as it is made as the mixture quickly loses bulk if kept standing. Once cooled, store in an airtight container for up to 2 days to prevent the cake from drying out.

As soon as egg whites are stiff gradually whisk in remaining sugar. Sprinkle ground almonds over egg whites and carefully fold in, using a large metal tablespoon, until only just combined.

MOIST RICH CHOCOLATE CAKE

For ingredients, pan sizes and timings, see chart.

- Preheat oven to 160°C (325°F/Gas 3). Line and grease a cake tin (pan), see page 9. Put the milk in a jug and add the vinegar. Set aside while preparing cake mixture.
- Melt chocolate, see page 16. Combine margarine, sugar and eggs in a bowl. Sift together flour, bicarbonate of soda (baking soda) and the cocoa (unsweetened cocoa powder). Add to bowl with half the milk.
- Using a wooden spoon or electric mixer, beat until smooth. Add melted chocolate and beat again until ingredients are combined.
- Scrape mixture into prepared tin (pan). Bake at once (see Expert Advice, page 40) for time stated in chart. A skewer inserted in the centre should come out clean. Cool in tin for 30 minutes, then transfer to a wire rack, Remove lining paper.

MOIST RICH CHOCOLATE CAKE - QUANTITIES CHART

Ingredients	Tin (Pan) Size		
	15cm (6 in) round or 13cm (5 in) square	20cm (8 in) round or 18cm(7 in) square	25cm (10 in) round or 23cm (9 in) square
milk	125ml (4 fl oz/$^1/_2$ cup)	250ml (8 fl oz/1 cup)	470ml (15 fl oz/1$^3/_4$ cups)
vinegar	1 tsp	1 tbsp	2 tbsp
chocolate, plain (semisweet)	60g (2 oz/ 2 squares)	125g (4 oz/4 squares)	250g (8 oz/8 squares)
margarine, soft	60g (2 oz)	125g (4 oz)	250g (8 oz)
sugar, caster (superfine)	125g (4 oz/$^1/_2$ cup)	250g (8 oz/1 cup)	500g (1 lb/2 cups)
eggs	1	2	4
flour, self-raising	155g (5oz/1$^1/_4$ cups)	315g (10 oz/2$^1/_2$ cups)	685g (1 lb 6oz/5$^1/_2$ cups)
bicarbonate of soda (baking soda)	$^1/_2$ tsp	1 tsp	2 tsp
cocoa	1 tbsp	2 tbsp	4 tbsp
Baking Time	1 hour	1$^1/_2$ hours	2$^1/_4$ hours

CHOCOLATE FUDGE CAKE

*F*lavoured with cocoa (unsweetened cocoa powder), Chocolate Fudge Cake has a very rich, dense texture. Top it with Chocolate Fudge Icing on page 29 or Ganache, see page 28. The cake is particularly thick, so use a deep sturdy tin (pan). If you prefer a shallower cake, use a 23 or 25cm (9 or 10 in) tin.

250g (8 oz) butter, softened, or soft margarine
375g (12 oz/2 cups) soft dark brown sugar
375g (12 oz/ 3 cups) plain (all–purpose) flour
1 tbsp baking powder
4 eggs, lightly beaten
4 tbsp golden syrup (light corn syrup)
125g (4 oz/1 cup) cocoa
(unsweetened cocoa powder)
185ml (6 fl oz/³/₄ cup) warm water
155ml (1/4 pt/²/₃ cup) plain yogurt

● Preheat oven to 150°C (300°F/Gas 2). Grease and fully line a 20cm (8 in) round cake tin (pan) or 18cm (7 in) square tin, see page 9.
● Combine butter or margarine and sugar in a large bowl and beat, using a wooden spoon or electric mixer, until pale and fluffy. Sift flour and baking powder together in a separate bowl.
● Gradually add beaten eggs to creamed mixture, beating well after each addition. A tablespoon of flour added to the mixture will prevent curdling.
● Stir in syrup. In a small bowl, blend cocoa (unsweetened cocoa powder) with measured water to make a paste. Beat into mixture in large bowl.

● Add flour mixture and yogurt, following detailed instructions below. Scrape into prepared tin (pan) and level surface. Bake for 1¹/₄–1¹/₂ hours or until well risen. A skewer inserted in the centre of the cake should come out clean. Cool briefly in tin, then invert on a wire rack and leave to cool completely. Remove lining paper.

EXPERT ADVICE

≈

Soured cream may be used instead of the yogurt, and treacle (molasses or dark corn syrup) substituted for the golden syrup (light corn syrup) for an even darker cake.

Using a large metal tablespoon, fold in half the sifted flour and baking powder mixture, using a figure–of–eight action. Fold in yogurt, then add remaining flour in the same way as before, until only just combined.

BASIC TECHNIQUES

MELTING CHOCOLATE

To achieve good results with chocolate it is important to melt it correctly. This is crucial if it is to be used for decorating purposes such as piping leaves and runouts, or for swirling over a cake. Chocolate which has been overheated may develop discoloured streaking or a mottled appearance once set.

Break chocolate into small pieces and place in a heatproof bowl. Bring a saucepan of water to the boil, then remove from the heat. Place the bowl of chocolate over the pan, above the water level. Leave the chocolate until completely melted. Stir lightly before use.

MELTING CHOCOLATE IN THE MICROWAVE

While the microwave is perfect for melting chocolate for mousses, puddings, cake mixtures and icings, care must be taken when melting chocolate for decorative work, as the temperature is difficult to control. Chocolate heated in the microwave retains its shape and should be tested with a fork. Break the chocolate into pieces and place in a suitable bowl. Heat on Medium power, allowing 3 minutes for 185-250g (6–8 oz/6–8 squares) chocolate. Leave to stand in microwave for 5 minutes; reheat briefly if necessary.

COVERING A CAKE WITH MELTED CHOCOLATE

Melted chocolate makes an easy cake covering. For a 20cm (8 in) layer cake you will need 250g (8 oz/8 squares) chocolate. Follow step–by step instructions right.

~ 1 ~

Place cake on a serving plate. Lightly stir melted chocolate, then pour it over the cake. Using a palette knife, swiftly spread chocolate evenly over top and down sides of cake to cover it completely.

~ 2 ~

As chocolate cools, lightly swirl surface with a clean palette knife. Alternatively, run serrated edge of a plastic cake decorating scraper over surface. Leave cake in a cool place to set.

MAKING A PAPER PIPING BAG

*I*t is very useful to be able to make your own piping bags. Use good quality greaseproof paper (parchment). Follow the simple step–by–step instructions right. Finished bags can be fitted with piping tubes (tips). Alternatively, snip the end of the bag to make a hole of the required size; for plain icing snip a small piece straight across pointed end of cone. For flowers make a diagonal cut, and for leaves cut either side to form a small 'V'.

QUICK TIPS

❖

● Use clean, dry bowls for melting chocolate. Grease or moisture will spoil the texture.

● When pouring melted chocolate from a bowl, first wipe underside of bowl to prevent drips of condensation from touching chocolate.

● Chocolate marks very easily, so try to avoid touching decorations with your hands. Where possible use a piece of soft cloth or gloves to pick up pieces of chocolate work. If you must use your hands, run them under the cold tap.

● If unused to piping chocolate, practise on greaseproof paper (parchment) before working on the cake.

● If chocolate starts to harden in a piping bag, it can be softened by reheating in the microwave for several seconds providing no metal piping tube (tip) has been used.

● On a hot day, avoid doing delicate chocolate work. It can be very difficult to handle.

● Keep leftover chocolate that has hardened in a bowl or bag. It can be stored for melting a second time.

~ 1 ~

Cut a 25 x 20 cm (10 x 8 in) rectangle from good quality greaseproof paper (parchment). Cut paper in half diagonally and place one piece flat on table with small point nearest to you. Fold right-hand point over to centre to make a cone.

~ 2 ~

Holding cone in position with thumb and first finger of left hand, lift paper off table. Pick up final point with right hand and wrap over cone so all three points meet together underneath. Fold points over twice to secure cone.

CHOCOLATE CARAQUE & CURLS

*G*iven a little time, highly professional looking scrolls or chocolate caraque can be made for decorating a cake, gâteau or chocolate dessert. For everyday cakes, press pared curls or grated chocolate around the sides, as for the Milky Marble Cake illustrated on page 43. Once made, caraque and curls quickly soften, so should be kept in a very cool place.

CARAQUE

Melt 250g (8 oz/8 squares) plain (semisweet) chocolate and pour onto a marble slab or other clean smooth surface. Leave until set.

Use a long knife with a rigid blade. Hold knife at angle of 45° to the chocolate. Draw it lightly across to cut thin layers that curl into scrolls. Carefully transfer scrolls to a plate or tray and keep cool while making remainder.

Fans are made by the same process, but use the end of a round–bladed knife.

CURLS

Using a potato peeler, pare away curls from a bar or slab of plain (semisweet) chocolate, milk (German sweet) or white chocolate. As when making caraque, if the chocolate is too cold it may be brittle. Leave in a warm place for a few minutes, or heat very briefly in the microwave before trying again.

GRATED CHOCOLATE

Grated chocolate is useful for melting into sauces or as a speedy alternative to curls for decorating the sides of a cake. Use the coarse blades of a metal grater.

EXPERT ADVICE
≈

If the chocolate fails to come away in scrolls, try adjusting the angle of the knife. If too cold, the chocolate may break off in brittle pieces. Leave in a warm place for a few minutes before trying again.

CHOCOLATE CUTOUTS & BOXES

*M*elted chocolate can be thinly spread on greaseproof paper (parchment) and left to set, ready for cutting out numerous novelty shapes or dainty boxes. A simple cake for a child's birthday could be made by cutting out milk (semisweet) chocolate shapes and securing them to a cake covered in white chocolate. Squares or panels of chocolate can also be made for covering the tops or sides of cakes, a technique which has been used to good effect on the Chequered Chocolate Parcel illustrated on page 57 and the White Chocolate Box illustrated on page 33.

CHOCOLATE CUTOUTS

Melt plain (semisweet), milk (German sweet) or white chocolate in a bowl over hot water. Pour onto a sheet of greaseproof paper (parchment) or wax paper.

Spread chocolate with a knife to thinly cover the paper. Gently lift up the paper at the edges and shake lightly so that the chocolate forms a smooth layer.

Leave in a cool place until set. Using metal biscuit (cookie) cutters, cut out shapes and lift away from the paper.

CHOCOLATE BOXES

These can be made in miniature *petit four* sizes or slightly larger for individual cakes. For each box cut out five equal squares of chocolate, each 2.5cm (1 in) in diameter. Place one square on surface and cover with 1cm (1/2 in) square of chocolate sponge. Spread a little whipped cream or Ganache, see page 28, over the sponge, then secure the four remaining squares around the cream to make a box. Finish with strawberries or other fresh fruit and sprigs of mint or chocolate leaves. For larger chocolate boxes increase the size of squares to 4cm (1 1/2 in) and use 2.5cm (1 in) squares of sponge.

MODELLING CHOCOLATE

*M*odelling chocolate is made from a mixture of chocolate and liquid glucose. Very easy to manage, it can be shaped into stunning flowers, figures, ribbons and novelty shapes. On these two pages you will find simple instructions for modelling roses, teddy bears and fir cones, but with a little practice the possibilities are endless, particularly if a mixture of plain (semisweet), milk (German sweet) and white chocolate is used. To make 155g (5 oz) modelling chocolate you will need 125g (4 oz/4 squares) chocolate and 2 tbsp liquid glucose.

Melt the chocolate in a heatproof bowl over hot water. Remove from the heat and beat in the glucose until a paste is formed which comes away from the sides of the bowl. Place the paste in a polythene bag and chill for about 1 hour until firm but pliable. See also Expert Advice, page 58.

CHOCOLATE ROSES

*T*o make a chocolate rose, take a piece of modelling chocolate about the size of a grape; shape into a cone. Press down on the surface and squeeze a 'waist' into the cone near the base. Take another piece of paste about half the size of the cone and press it as flat as possible to create a petal shape. Secure this around the cone. Shape another slightly larger petal and wrap this around the first, overlapping it slightly. Continue building up the rose, making each petal slightly larger than the previous one, until you have a complete rose of 7–8 petals, as illustrated below. Bend and tuck the outer petals to create a realistic shape. Once completed, slice just below the petals; use the base to shape the next cone. To create a posy, vary the sizes of the roses. For buds use just 3–4 petals, tucking them tightly around the cone.

CHOCOLATE TEDDY BEARS

A group of chocolate teddy bears in various sizes would make a lovely decoration for a child's birthday cake. For contrast, some teddies could be made from dark paste and finished with white.

Roll a piece of white modelling chocolate to a ball about the size of a plum. Gently press onto surface. Roll and position a smaller ball for head. Shape two flat rounds of paste. Halve one and position for ears; use the other to make a muzzle. Shape two arms and legs as illustrated below; secure in position. Use small pads of plain (semisweet) or milk (German sweet) modelling chocolate to complete the paws, feet and centres of ears. Use more dark paste to complete facial features.

CHOCOLATE FIR CONES

C hocolate fir cones in various sizes would be appropriate for a winter birthday cake or an alternative Christmas cake. Use the chocolate basket illustrated on page 55, packing it with fir cones and finishing it with bows of red or green ribbon. Mini fir cones would look good on a Yule log. To shape a cone, mould a large piece of modelling chocolate to an egg shape, with pointed end at top. Very lightly dust the thick end of a piping tube (tip) with cornflour (cornstarch). Starting near base of cone, press end of tube into paste to imitate the scales of the cone. Continue up the sides of the cone, overlapping the semi–circular scales and making them smaller near the top than at the bottom.

PIPING CHOCOLATE

There are many interesting chocolate decorations that can be made by piping directly onto the cake. Alternatively, decorations may be piped onto paper and transferred to the cake when hardened. Decorations include simple chocolate lace, as used on the Mocha Gateau on page 52, runouts, see facing page, or the designs below.

It is slightly more difficult to pipe melted chocolate than chocolate icing, as chocolate has a softer consistency and can be difficult to release from the tube (tip) when a design is completed. Chocolate buttercream is far easier to pipe than melted chocolate, but can only be piped directly onto a cake.

Most simple chocolate piping is done with a medium writing tube (tip) or a medium star tube (tip). Greaseproof paper (parchment) bags are easier to use than fabric ones – see page 17 for how to make them.

STARS AND SCALLOPS Use chocolate buttercream in a paper piping bag fitted with a star tube (tip). Pipe around top edge or base of cake.

DOTS Use melted chocolate in a paper piping bag fitted with a writing tube (tip). Pipe random dots over a cake covered with Chocolate Moulding Icing, see page 27.

SNAILTRAIL Use melted chocolate in a paper piping bag fitted with a writing tube (tip). Pipe a line of fine beading around the base of a celebration chocolate cake.

CORNELLI WORK This is a method of piping in controlled wavy lines. It is piped directly onto the cake and is particularly useful for hiding cracks and imperfections in chocolate icing. Use melted chocolate in a paper piping bag fitted with a writing tube (tip) and pipe a long continuous curvy line over the cake surface.

EXPERT ADVICE

≈

If you find the chocolate too runny to pipe successfully, try adding a few drops of glycerol (glycerine).

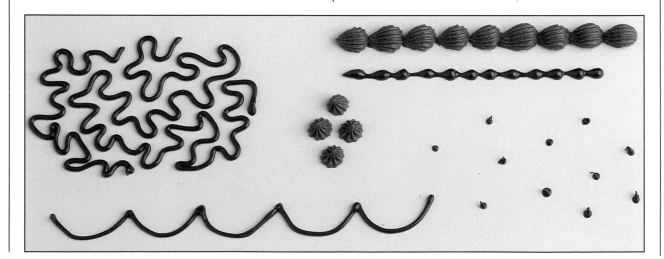

CHOCOLATE RUNOUTS

Chocolate runouts can be made in almost any shape. Templates for simple designs are given on page 71, but you can trace designs from greeting cards or books or even make up your own. If experimenting for the first time, it is best to stick to simple shapes.

● Trace the chosen design. Secure each tracing to a flat surface with wax paper on top.

● Place a little melted chocolate in a paper piping bag fitted with a writing tube (tip); pipe over outlines, making sure joins are neat. Set.

● Place more melted chocolate in a bag fitted with a clean tube (tip). Fill centres, following instructions below. When set, carefully pull paper away from runouts.

Working fairly quickly, fill in outline with melted chocolate, easing chocolate into corners with the tip of a cocktail stick (toothpick) if necessary. Cornelli work can be used if a lacy effect is preferred. Leave to set.

CHOCOLATE FOR DIPPING

Fresh and crystallized fruits, truffles and nuts make delectable decorations when dipped in chocolate. Nuts and truffles are best completely coated in chocolate, while fruits such as seedless grapes, strawberries and cherries look more attractive if half dipped. Nuts, truffles and crystallized fruits can be dipped several days in advance, but fresh fruits should be dipped on the day they are to be eaten. Before you start, wash and dry all fruit thoroughly. Line baking sheet with greaseproof paper (parchment) or wax paper. Melt plain (semisweet), milk (German sweet) or white chocolate, leaving bowl over a pan of hot water. Instructions for dipping are given below.

Holding fruit by its stalk or stalk end, half dip into chocolate and twist slightly. Allow excess chocolate to drip back into the bowl, then transfer fruit to paper to dry. Dip nuts one at a time; remove using a dipping fork.

CHOCOLATE LEAVES

These make some of the easiest yet most effective decorations for a chocolate cake, whether as a covering for the whole cake, as in the Christmas Wreath illustrated on page 47, or simply to complete an arrangement of chocolate roses. Virtually any non–poisonous leaf may be used as a mould. Rose, lemon balm, mint, bay leaves and holly all work extremely well. To cover about 20 leaves you will need 90g (3 oz/3 squares) plain (semisweet), milk (German sweet), dark dessert (German dark) chocolate or milk chocolate. Instructions for coating are given below.

Gently wipe leaves with a damp cloth. Using a clean paintbrush, thickly coat underside of each leaf with melted chocolate. Lay flat on wax paper, chocolate side up, until set, then carefully peel leaves off chocolate.

CHOCOLATE CASES

Small *petit four* or paper sweet cases (candy cups) make perfect moulds for shaping chocolate cases. These can be filled with piped Ganache, see page 28, used as a container for whipped cream or lemon mousse or scattered over a chocolate cake for decoration, as on the White Chocolate Box illustrated on page 33. They also make tasty containers for truffles. To coat about 20 paper sweet cases you will need 125g (4 oz/4 squares) plain (semisweet), milk (German sweet) or white chocolate, melted. Instructions for coating are given below.

Using the back of a small teaspoon thickly coat base and sides of paper cases (candy cups). Scoop out excess chocolate, then invert cases to set. When set check sides for any thinly coated areas; re–coat if necessary. Peel away paper.

The basic cakes on pages 10–15 can be transformed by the addition of these icings, pastes and fillings, all of which have been selected for their affinity with chocolate.

BUTTERCREAM

❖

Buttercream is an easy and versatile topping and filling. The plain version is ideal for everyday cakes, while the citrus–flavoured variation below is particularly suitable for chocolate cakes. For novelty cakes it can be coloured and piped. One of buttercream's many advantages is that it can be made in advance. Cover it closely, keep it chilled and soften it by whisking just before use.

90g (3 oz) butter, softened
185g (6 oz/1/1¼ cups) icing (confectioners')
sugar
1 tbsp hot water

Beat softened butter in a bowl with a wooden spoon or electric mixer until smooth. Sift in icing (confectioners') sugar. Gradually beat it into the butter. Add the water and continue beating until light and fluffy. Sufficient to fill a 20–23cm (8–9 in) layer cake. Double quantities to cover top and sides.

VARIATIONS

CHOCOLATE BUTTERCREAM Add 2 tbsp sifted cocoa (unsweetened cocoa powder) with the icing (confectioners') sugar.

CITRUS BUTTERCREAM Add finely grated rind of 1 orange or lemon to the butter.

EXPERT ADVICE

≈

When food colouring is added to buttercream the colour may be altered slightly because of the naturally creamy colour of the butter. If the colour is crucial, substitute white vegetable fat (shortening) for the butter.

GLACE ICING

❖

Glacé icing resembles a glaze. It cannot be piped, but makes an easy topping for simple chocolate cakes. It can be swirled with melted chocolate for a marbled effect, as the Milky Marble Cake illustrated on page 43, or flavoured with melted chocolate.

185g (6oz/1¼ cups) icing (confectioners') sugar
2–3 tsp warm water

Sift icing (confectioners') sugar into a small bowl. Gradually beat in water until icing thickly coats the back of the spoon. Use immediately or cover surface to prevent the formation of a crust. Sufficient to top a 20–23cm (8–9 in) cake.

VARIATIONS

CHOCOLATE GLACE ICING Melt 60g (2 oz/2 squares) plain (semisweet) chocolate and stir in 15g (1/2 oz) butter. Add to the glacé icing.

COFFEE GLACE ICING Mix the warm water with 1 tbsp instant coffee powder before adding to the icing (confectioners') sugar.

APRICOT GLAZE

❖

This is frequently brushed over cakes before they are covered with marzipan (almond paste). It is also used to stick cakes together.

125g (4 oz/$\frac{1}{2}$ cup) apricot jam
1 tbsp lemon juice

● Warm jam in a small saucepan until melted. Press through a sieve into a clean pan and stir in lemon juice.
● Boil for 30 seconds, then remove from heat. Cool slightly, then apply to cake with a clean brush. Makes about 125ml (4 fl oz/$\frac{1}{2}$ cup).

CHOCOLATE MARZIPAN

❖

Marzipan (almond paste) has several uses in cake decorating. It can be used to cover cakes before adding a layer of Chocolate Moulding Icing, see opposite, or used as an alternative to icing as on the Battenburg Cake illustrated on page 35. Pliable in texture, it can also be moulded into novelty shapes. The chocolate ribbon on page 57, roses on page 20 and teddy bears on page 21 can all be made in marzipan. The results will be slightly less delicate, but perfectly acceptable.

250g (8 oz/2 cups) ground almonds
125g (4 oz/$\frac{1}{2}$ cup) caster (superfine) sugar
125g (4 oz/$\frac{3}{4}$ cup) icing (confectioners') sugar
45g (1$\frac{1}{2}$ oz/$\frac{1}{3}$ cup) cocoa
(unsweetened cocoa powder)
2 egg whites
1 tsp lemon juice

● Place almonds and both sugars in a large bowl. Sift cocoa (unsweetened cocoa powder) into the bowl and stir the ingredients together. Add egg whites and lemon juice and mix until mixture starts to bind together. Complete, following detailed instructions below.
● When ready, wrap marzipan in foil or a polythene bag. Store in a cool place, or refrigerate for up to 3 days before using. Makes about 500g (1 lb).

VARIATIONS

PLAIN MARZIPAN (Almond Paste) Make as above, omitting the cocoa (unsweetened cocoa powder) and using only 1 egg white.
CHOCOLATE HAZELNUT PASTE Make as above, substituting grounds hazelnuts for almonds.

As soon as mixture starts to form a paste, turn it out on a surface dusted with icing (confectioners') sugar. Knead paste lightly until completely smooth. Avoid over kneading which would make the paste soft and oily.

CHOCOLATE MOULDING ICING

❖

This resembles ordinary moulding icing or sugarpaste and is equally versatile, whether used to cover a smart, special occasion cake or a novelty one. It can be made using plain (semisweet), dark dessert (German dark), milk (German sweet) or white chocolate.

*185g (6 oz/6 squares) plain
(semisweet) chocolate
2 tbsp liquid glucose
1 egg white
500g (1 lb/3 cups) icing (confectioners') sugar,
sifted*

Break up the chocolate and place it in a small heatproof bowl over a saucepan of hot water.

Beat chocolate mixture until smooth, gradually adding remaining icing (confectioners') sugar. When mixture becomes too stiff to beat, turn it onto a surface and knead in remaining icing sugar to make a stiff paste.

Add the liquid glucose and leave until melted. Remove from the heat and leave for 2 minutes, then add the egg white and a little of the icing (confectioners') sugar. Beat with an electric mixer until smooth, following detailed instructions below left. Finally, wrap the paste in cling film (plastic wrap) or a polythene bag and keep in a cool place for up to 3 days. Sufficient to cover a 20–23cm (8–9 in) cake.

EXPERT ADVICE

≈

For successful rolling and moulding, Chocolate Moulding Icing must be the correct consistency. If when rolled it becomes soft and sticks to the work surface, gather it up and knead in more icing (confectioners') sugar. If the icing is dry and cracks, heat it in the microwave on High for 30 seconds. If it remains dry, sprinkle with water and knead again to soften.

Unlike ordinary sugarpaste, Chocolate Moulding Icing does not develop a dry crust if exposed to the air for more than a minute or two. It does, however, harden slowly as the chocolate sets. If this happens, heat it in the microwave on High for 30 seconds. Allow to stand for 1 minute, then microwave for a further 30 seconds if necessary. When rolling or moulding the icing, dust surface and hands with cornflour (cornstarch) to prevent sticking.

GANACHE

There are several recipes for Chocolate Ganache, one of which includes liqueur (see *Simple Cakes: Icings & Frostings* in the *Sugarcraft Skills Series*), but all result in a deliciously smooth and creamy mixture which makes an irresistible filling or covering for special occasion chocolate cakes. Freshly made ganache has a pouring consistency. It thickens as it cools. For a smooth cake covering, use when the ganache thickly coats the back of the spoon. If left until completely cold and whisked, it becomes thick enough to use as a cake filling. It may also be piped into chocolate cases such as those illustrated on page 24, to make delicious petits fours. Plain (semisweet) or dark dessert (German dark) chocolate gives a rich, dark ganache, but milk (German sweet) or white chocolate may be substituted.

*250g (8 oz/8 squares) plain
(semisweet) chocolate
155ml (¹/₄pt/²/₃ cup) double (heavy) cream*

Melt chocolate in a heatproof bowl over hot water. Place cream in a small heavy–bottomed saucepan and bring just to the boil. Complete following detailed instructions above right. Sufficient to cover top and sides of a 20–23cm (8–9 in) cake.

EXPERT ADVICE
≈
For filling cakes and piping, cold ganache can be whisked with an electric mixer until paler in colour and increased in volume.

Slowly pour hot cream over chocolate, beating well with a balloon whisk until cream is incorporated and mixture is completely smooth. Chill, stirring occasionally, until ganache has reached the required consistency.

CREAMY CHOCOLATE FROSTING

A tangy icing based on cream cheese, this makes an interesting alternative to more traditional fillings for chocolate sponges or nutty chocolate cakes.

*125g (4 oz/ ²/₃ cup) full fat cream cheese
50g (2 oz/2 squares) plain
(semisweet) chocolate, melted
60g (2 oz/ ¹/₃ cup) icing (confectioners') sugar*

Place cream cheese in a bowl and beat with a wooden spoon to soften. Beat in melted chocolate, then icing (confectioners') sugar until smooth. Sufficient to fill a 20cm (8 in) sandwich cake. Use double quantities if cake is to be topped as well as filled.

CHOCOLATE FROSTING

❖

*60g (2 oz/2 squares) plain
(semisweet) chocolate
185g (6 oz/ ³/₄ cup) caster (superfine) sugar
1 egg white
pinch of cream of tartar*

Melt the chocolate in a heatproof bowl over hot water. Combine the sugar, egg white and cream of tartar in a large heatproof bowl. Place the bowl over a saucepan of gently simmering water. Using an electric mixer beat ingredients together until mixture forms soft peaks. This will take 6–8 minutes. Continue, following instructions below. Sufficient to cover an 18–20cm (7–8 in) cake.

CHOCOLATE FUDGE ICING

❖

A thick covering of this rich icing can liven up a plain chocolate cake. Swirl it over the cake while still soft.

*250g (8 oz/8 squares) plain
(semisweet) chocolate
125g (4 oz) butter
2 eggs
250g (8 oz/1¹/₂ cups) icing (confectioners')
sugar, sifted*

Break up chocolate and melt it with butter in a heatproof bowl over a saucepan of hot water. Stir, leave the mixture to cool for 5 minutes, then continue, following instructions below. Sufficient to cover a 20-23cm (8–9 in) cake.

Remove bowl from heat. Gradually whisk melted chocolate into egg whites until evenly incorporated. Immediately spread frosting over top and sides of cake, using a palette knife to spread and swirl mixture.

Add eggs to cooled chocolate mixture. Beat well. Add sifted icing (confectioners') sugar, beating until smooth. Continue beating until mixture almost holds its shape. If icing remains too thin, chill until thickened.

CHOCOLATE CREME PATISSIERE

❖

Rich chocolate custards stabilized with cornflour (cornstarch) make delicious fillings for light chocolate sponges or roulades. The basic mixture can be flavoured with white or dark chocolate.

125g (4 oz/ ¹/₂ cup) caster (superfine) sugar
30g (1 oz/ 3 tbsp) cornflour (cornstarch)
4 egg yolks
1 tsp vanilla essence (extract)
625ml (1 pt/2¹/₂ cups) milk
60g (2 oz/2 squares) chocolate, grated

Mix sugar, cornflour (cornstarch), egg yolks, vanilla and a little of the milk in a bowl until smooth. Bring remaining milk to the boil in a saucepan. Pour onto egg yolk mixture, beating well. Return to saucepan. Complete recipe following instructions above right. Sufficient to fill a roulade or Swiss (jelly) roll. Halve quantities to fill a 20–23cm (8–9 in) sandwich cake.

CHOCOLATE CREME PATISSIERE *Bring mixture to the boil, stirring constantly until very thick and smooth. Off heat, beat in grated chocolate. Press through a sieve into a bowl. Cover with greaseproof paper (parchment) to prevent formation of a skin.*

EXPERT ADVICE

≈

In addition to using Chocolate Crème Pâtissière as a filling for cakes, try it in cream horns, chocolate éclairs and cream puffs. Use it also as a filling for tarts and tartlets, particularly those topped with glazed fruit.

CREME DIPLOMATE

❖

3 tsp custard powder or 4 tsp cornflour (cornstarch)
1 tbsp caster (superfine) sugar
155ml (¹/₄pt/²/₃ cup) milk
155ml (¹/₄ pt/²/₃ cup) double (heavy) cream
few drops of vanilla essence (extract)

Blend custard powder or cornflour (cornstarch) and sugar with a little milk in a saucepan. Stir in remaining milk and cook over moderate heat, stirring constantly, until thick and smooth. Pour into a bowl, cover and chill. Whip double (heavy) cream until thick and fold into chilled custard with vanilla. Makes about 315ml (¹/₂ pt/1¹/₄ cups).

CHOCOLATE TRUFFLES

Set in paper sweet cases (candy cups) and attractively boxed, truffles make a very acceptable gift – an idea which has been taken one step further in the White Chocolate Box cake illustrated on page 33. The quantity below makes about 12 truffles. Alternatively, the truffle paste makes a delicious cake filling, see Expert Advice.

125g (4 oz/4 squares) plain (semisweet), milk (German sweet) or white chocolate
3 tbsp double (heavy) cream
1 tbsp brandy, rum or orange–flavoured liqueur
60g (2 oz/¹/₃ cup) icing (confectioners') sugar

C O A T I N G

use any of the following: finely grated chocolate, chocolate vermicelli (sprinkles), cocoa (unsweetened cocoa powder), icing (confectioners') sugar, shredded coconut

● Break up chocolate. Put it in a small, heavy–bottomed saucepan. Add cream. Heat very gently, stirring frequently until chocolate has melted and mixture is smooth and thick. Remove from heat and beat in liqueur and icing (confectioners') sugar. Allow to cool to room temperature.

● Using a coffee spoon or small teaspoon shape chocolate mixture into small balls. Coat in chosen coating, following detailed instructions below.

V A R I A T I O N S

CHOCOLATE-DIPPED TRUFFLES Make chocolate balls as above, arrange them on baking sheets covered in greaseproof paper (parchment) and chill until firm. Melt about 90g (3 oz/3 squares) plain (semisweet) chocolate in a bowl. Add chocolate balls one at a time to melted chocolate; turn gently until coated. Lift truffle on dipping fork, tapping fork gently against side of bowl to drain excess chocolate. Transfer to a tray lined with greaseproof paper. While chocolate is still soft, texture truffles with fork. Leave truffles on paper until dry.

Place chosen coatings on flat plates and roll truffles until evenly coated. Place in refrigerator until firm.

EXPERT ADVICE

≈

Truffle paste firms up once made, but should be used before it sets completely. It makes a good cake filling. Try it with the Moist Rich Chocolate Cake on page 14 or the Chocolate Fudge Cake on page 15. The quantity above is sufficient to fill a 20–23cm (8–9 in) cake.

WHITE CHOCOLATE BOX

*S*ome of the techniques outlined earlier in this book are used on this pretty chocolate box. The discarded 'paper' cases are in fact made from white chocolate, and the truffles make a delicious addition.

3–egg chocolate–flavoured Genoese Sponge mixture, see page 11
440g (14 oz/14 squares) white chocolate
470ml (³/₄pt/2 cups) double (heavy) cream
3 tbsp Amaretto liqueur
DECORATION
16 large Brazil nuts
10–12 Truffles rolled in grated white chocolate, see page 31
12 silver sugared almonds
12 gold sugared almonds
1m (1 yd 3 in) gold–or silver–trimmed pink ribbon, about 1cm (¹/₂ in) wide

● Preheat oven to 180°C (350°F/Gas 4). Bake cake in base lined and greased 18cm (7 in) square cake tin (pan). Cool on a wire rack. Remove lining paper.

● Draw a 23 x 18.5cm (9 x 7¹/₄ in) rectangle on a sheet of wax paper. Melt half the white chocolate, spoon it onto the paper and spread with a palette knife to just cover the marked rectangle. Shake paper to level chocolate, using the technique described on page 19. Leave until set.

● Melt the remaining white chocolate and use some of it to dip the Brazil nuts as described on page 23. Use the rest to make 12 chocolate petit four cases, following the technique on page 24. Leave to set.

● Using a long serrated knife, cut the cake horizontally in half. Place one half on a flat serving plate. Combine the cream and liqueur in a bowl and whisk to soft peaks. Use to fill and cover the cake, as described in Step 1 on page 34.

● Trim the white chocolate rectangle to precisely 23 x 18.5cm (9 x 7¹/₄ in), using a clean ruler and a sharp knife. Cut the rectangle into 4 equal panels, each measuring 5.75 x 18.5cm (2¹/₄ x 7¹/₄ in). Secure these around the sides of the cake, following instructions in Step 2 on page 34.

● Finally, decorate the cake and board, following steps 3–4 on page 34.

EXPERT ADVICE

≈

Make the cake, chocolate box panels and decorations several days in advance, but do not assemble the cake until the day of serving or the cream will deteriorate.

For a quick version use bought white chocolates, arranging them uniformly in chocolate or paper cases – a delectable gift for a chocolate-lover.

~ 1 ~

Spread about a third of the whipped cream over the cake. Gently rest second half on top. Use a palette knife to spread more cream thickly over sides of cake. Spread remaining cream over the top, smoothing it lightly.

~ 2 ~

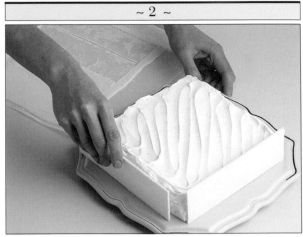

Carefully peel wax paper away from the chocolate panels. Place one panel against the side of cake and press gently into place. Complete box effect by fixing remaining panels in place so that edges meet neatly at corners.

~ 3 ~

Scatter most of the chocolate-coated Brazil nuts, truffles and chocolate cases over top of cake. Arrange silver and gold sugared almonds over the chocolate decorations in an apparently random but neat arrangement.

~ 4 ~

Scatter remaining truffles, cases and nuts beside cake on plate or board. Tie ribbon neatly around cake, securing it with a dot of melted chocolate. Keep cake cool; serve the same day.

Battenburg, see page 36

BATTENBURG

Illustrated on previous page

*T*his recipe presents a traditional cake in a novel way with miniature marzipan (almond paste) Battenburg slices scattered over and around the cake.

Quick Mix Cake mixture, see page 11
pink food colouring
1 tbsp cocoa (unsweetened cocoa powder)
1 tbsp boiling water
ASSEMBLY AND DECORATION
1 quantity Apricot Glaze, see page 26
1 quantity Chocolate Marzipan (almond paste),
see page 26
1/2 quantity plain Marzipan (almond paste),
see page 26
icing (confectioners') sugar for dusting
20cm (8 in) cake board

● Preheat oven to 160°C (325°F/Gas 3). Using card (see Expert Advice), divide an 18cm (7 in) square cake tin (pan) into two equal halves, securing card at ends with tape. Line and grease each half.

● Divide cake mixture equally between two bowls and beat a few drops of pink food colouring into one of them. (Do not make mixture too pink as colour will deepen during cooking.) Mix cocoa and water together and beat into remaining bowl of mixture. Spoon mixture into tin, following instructions in Step 1 opposite. Bake for about 40 minutes until firm. Cool; remove lining paper.

● Trim , cut up and assemble cakes with some of the apricot glaze, following instructions in Step 2 opposite.

● Knead a small piece of the chocolate marzipan (almond paste) into a quarter of the plain marzipan until it is the same colour as the chocolate cake. Colour remaining plain marzipan same shade of pink as cake.

● Roll out two thirds of the pink marzipan (almond paste) as thinly as possible on a surface dusted with icing (confectioners') sugar. Lightly dampen cake board. Lay pink marzipan over board and trim off excess.

● Mould cake–coloured and remaining pink marzipan (almond paste) into two blocks, each about 10 x 2.5 x 1cm (4 x 1 x 1/2 in). Cut up and assemble into miniature Battenburg as for the cake. Trim long sides of both marzipan and cake Battenburg to give neat edges. Brush long sides of cake with remaining glaze.

● Lightly knead three quarters of the remaining chocolate marzipan (almond paste). Roll out on a sheet of wax paper to a rectangle, about 36 x 20 cm (14 x 8 in). Use to cover long sides of cakes, as described in Steps 3–4 opposite. Use remaining chocolate marzipan to cover miniature Battenburg in the same way.

● Carefully transfer cake to covered board, making sure that join is underneath. Cut miniature Battenburg in 1 cm (1/2 in) slices and scatter them over the top and on the board.

EXPERT ADVICE

≈

The basic cake can be made several days in advance and stored in an airtight container before assembling. Trim the end of the cake after storing. The card used to separate the cake tin (pan) need not be strong. Part of a cereal packet is ideal.

~ 1 ~

Spoon chocolate cake mixture into one side of tin (pan) and level surface. Carefully spoon pink–coloured cake mixture into other side. Level surface.

~ 2 ~

Level cakes by cutting off domed tops. Slice each cake in half lengthways. Brush top of one pink cake generously with apricot glaze; top with chocolate cake. Repeat with remaining cakes, reversing colours, then stick cakes together.

~ 3 ~

Place cake on chocolate marzipan (almond paste). Using a knife, trim off excess marzipan at both ends of cake. Neaten untrimmed ends, making sure there is sufficient marzipan to cover sides and meet over top of cake.

~ 4 ~

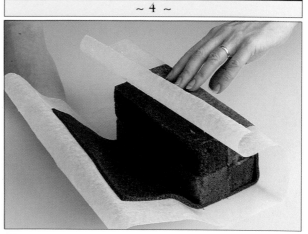

Using wax paper as a guide, bring marzipan (almond paste) up over cake until it meets in the middle. Join ends together, trimming off any excess paste. To give a neat finish, cut a thin slice from either end of the cake.

WHITE CHOCOLATE ROULADE

*T*his wonderfully moist cake is perfect for tea time. Plain (semisweet) chocolate may be used instead of white.

1 Chocolate Roulade made with white chocolate, see page 12
caster (superfine) sugar for dusting
60g (2 oz/¹/₂ cup) hazelnuts
50g (2 oz/¹/₂ cup) cold chocolate Créme Pâtissière made with white chocolate, see page 30
icing (confectioners') sugar for dusting
pink food colouring
pink roses, optional, to decorate

● Bake chocolate roulade and leave to cool in tin (pan). Invert onto a sheet of greaseproof paper (parchment) dusted with caster (superfine) sugar. Remove lining paper, then invert cake onto a second piece of greaseproof paper so crust faces upwards. Trim all edges.

● Roughly chop hazelnuts and brown under a moderate grill until lightly toasted. Leave to cool, then beat into créme pâtissiére. Fill and roll up roulade, following instructions right.

● Put a little icing (confectioners') sugar in a bowl. Add a few drops of food colour (or dots of paste) and work in, using the back of a teaspoon. Continue working in colour until sugar is pale pink.

● Dust a flat rectangular serving plate generously with some white icing (confectioners') sugar, then with pink sugar. Position roulade on plate and dust with more sugar. Decorate with pink roses, if desired.

Using a large palette knife spread the crème pâtissière over the roulade to within 1cm (¹/₂ in) of edges. Starting from a short side, and using the greaseproof paper (parchment) as a guide, carefully roll up roulade.

CHOCOLATE HEART

*F*lavoured with liqueur and decorated with chocolate leaves and luxurious candied fruits, this cake is perfect for a special occasion. Fresh fruits may be used instead of candied, if preferred, but should only be added just before serving.

2–egg Moist Rich Chocolate Cake mixture,
see page 14
4 tbsp brandy or orange–flavoured liqueur
COATING AND DECORATION
1 quantity Apricot Glaze, see page 26
500g (1 lb) plain Marzipan (almond paste),
see page 26
icing (confectioners') sugar for dusting
315g (10 oz/10 squares) plain (semisweet)
chocolate
125g (4 oz/4 squares) milk (German sweet)
chocolate, melted
185g (6 oz) mixed candied (glacé) fruit

● Preheat oven to 160°C (325°F/Gas 3). Bake cake in base lined and greased 25cm (10 in) heart–shaped tin (pan) for about 1½ hours or until a skewer inserted into the centre comes out clean. Cool. Remove lining paper.
● Invert cake on a large flat serving plate or heart–shaped cake board. Drizzle with brandy or orange–flavoured liqueur.

EXPERT ADVICE

≈

The Moist Rich Chocolate Cake should be baked immediately after mixing as soda is activated on being combined with liquid.

● Brush apricot glaze over top and sides of cake. Roll out marzipan (almond paste) to a round, 30cm (12 in) in diameter, on a surface lightly dusted with icing (confectioners') sugar. Lift over cake and ease to fit around sides. Trim off excess marzipan around base of cake.
● Melt plain (semisweet) chocolate and pour over cake; spread to cover top and sides. (See page 16 for technique.) Keep in a cool place until set.
● Melt milk (German sweet) chocolate and place a little in a paper piping bag fitted with a medium writing tube (tip). Use to decorate cake, following detailed instructions below.
● Use remaining melted milk (German sweet) chocolate to half–dip fruits, see page 23, and to make about 8 chocolate rose leaves, see page 24. When chocolate has set, arrange fruit and leaves over top of cake.

Holding piping bag about 5cm (2 in) above cake, pipe continuous fine lacy lines by moving your hand quickly over cake. To cover sides, tilt plate or board slightly with free hand and work with bag nearer surface of cake.

MILKY MARBLE CAKE

A simple teatime cake, marbled in both sponge and icing.

Madeira Cake mixture, see page 12
2 tbsp cocoa (unsweetened cocoa powder)
1 tbsp boiling water
1 tsp vanilla essence (extract)
grated rind of 1 lemon
ICING AND DECORATION
220g (7 oz/ 7 squares) milk (German sweet) chocolate
125g (4 oz/³/₄ cup) icing (confectioners') sugar
1 tbsp lemon juice

● Preheat oven to 160°C (325°F/Gas 3). Base line and grease a 20cm (8 in) round cake tin (pan).

● Divide cake mixture between two bowls. Beat cocoa (unsweetened cocoa powder) and boiling water together and add to one bowl. Stir vanilla essence (extract) and lemon rind into remaining bowl.

● Put alternate spoonfuls of chocolate and lemon–flavoured mixture into tin (pan), occasionally drawing a skewer through the mixture. Bake for about 1¹/₂ hours or until a skewer inserted into the centre of the cake comes out clean. Cool on a wire rack. Remove lining paper.

● Using 90g (3 oz/3 squares) of the chocolate, make curls, following instructions on page 18. Spread curls out thickly on a sheet of greaseproof paper (parchment). Melt remaining chocolate and set 2 tbsp aside. Spread rest of melted chocolate around sides of marble cake.

● While chocolate is still soft, coat side of cake in chocolate curls. The easiest way to do this is to place one hand palm down on top of the cake and the other palm up underneath it. Turn cake and roll it lightly in the chocolate curls. Do not press heavily or the sides will be unevenly coated.

● Place cake on a serving plate. Sift icing (confectioners') sugar into a bowl. Add lemon juice and mix glacé icing to the consistency of pouring cream. Spoon glacé icing onto top of cake and marble icing following the instructions below.

Spread glacé icing to edges of cake. Drizzle reserved 2 tbsp melted chocolate over icing. While still soft, run the tip of a cocktail stick (toothpick) through chocolate and icing to create the marbled effect.

RICH CHOCOLATE FUDGE CAKE

A traditional recipe, deliciously rich and tasty. The chocolate caraque gives a highly professional–looking finish.

20cm (8 in) round Chocolate Fudge Cake,
see page 15

ICING AND DECORATION

155ml (¹/₄pt/²/₃ cup) double (heavy) cream
2 tsp icing (confectioners') sugar,
plus extra for dusting
1 quantity Chocolate Fudge Icing, see page 29
1 quantity chocolate caraque, see page 18

● Using a long serrated knife, split the cake in half horizontally. Place the bottom half on a flat serving plate. Combine cream and icing (confectioners') sugar in a bowl and whisk to soft peaks. Sandwich cake together.

● Using a palette knife, spread about half the Chocolate Fudge Icing around sides of cake. Spoon remaining icing over top. Spread icing to cover cake evenly, then use tip of palette knife to mark a diagonal line from centre of top of cake down to base, as illustrated opposite. Repeat at 1cm (¹/₂ in) intervals all around cake to give a neat finish.

● Carefully arrange some of the chocolate caraque on top of cake. Add remaining pieces, placing them at different angles to create an informal but symmetrical effect.

● Cut three strips of greaseproof paper (parchment), each about 2.5cm (1 in) wide. Lightly lay strips over caraque, then dust cake with icing (confectioners') sugar, following instructions right.

EXPERT ADVICE

≈

To save time, coarsely grated chocolate (see page 18) can be used instead of caraque. To ensure that chocolate curls stick to icing, position them while icing is still soft. Removing greaseproof paper (parchment) strips from cake requires steady hands. Lift strips off one by one.

Try to avoid moving cake once it has been dusted with icing (confectioners') sugar. If you have to transport it, take paper and sugar with you and complete cake when you reach your destination.

Put a little icing (confectioners') sugar in fine sieve or tea strainer and use to heavily dust the top of the cake. Carefully lift off greaseproof paper (parchment) strips to reveal contrast between dusted and plain areas.

CHRISTMAS WREATH

℘hocolate leaves and tartan bows turn a simple ring cake into a wreath which would make an attractive centrepiece for a Christmas buffet table. An equally successful summertime version could be made using rose, lemon balm and mint leaves coated with pink or yellow coloured chocolate, and sugar flowerbuds.

Chocolate Mousse Cake mixture, see page 13
ICING AND DECORATION
125g (4 oz/4 squares) white chocolate
green food colouring
60g (2 oz/2 squares) plain (semisweet)
chocolate
60g (2 oz/2 squares) milk
(German sweet) chocolate
60 rose, holly and bay leaves
1 quantity Chocolate Frosting, see page 29
1m (1 yd 3 in) green, red or tartan ribbon,
about 1cm (¹/₂ in) wide

● Preheat oven to 180°C (350°F/Gas 4). Bake cake in base–lined and greased 1.1 litre (2 pt/5 cup) ring tin (pan) for 40 minutes until surface is crusty. Leave to cool in tin (pan), then loosen edges and invert onto a wire rack. Remove lining paper.

● Melt white chocolate. Following Expert Advice right, colour half of it pale green. Melt remaining chocolate in separate bowls. Use all the chocolate to make a selection of rose, holly and bay chocolate leaves, see page 24.

● Place chocolate ring on a large serving plate and spread with frosting. While frosting is still soft, decorate with prepared leaves, following instructions below.

● Finally cut ribbon into three equal lengths, tie into bows and position on cake. Keep cake in a cool place until ready to serve.

EXPERT ADVICE

≈

White chocolate can easily be coloured in soft pastel shades to add interest to novelty cakes, leaves, cases, cutouts and runouts. After melting the chocolate in a bowl over hot water, stir in a little oil-based paste food colouring, or powder. Do not use water–based colouring, which will make the chocolate thicken and spoil.

Arrange prepared leaves attractively over cake, starting from outside edges and working towards centre. Try to arrange leaves in such a way that the different colours and types of leaf are evenly distributed.

CLOWN CAKE

A perfect cake for a small child's birthday. If you wish to add candles, press them into small balls of chocolate moulding icing. Attach them to the cake board.

double quantity Quick Mix Cake mixture,
see page 11
200g (7 oz/7 squares) plain (semisweet)
chocolate
ICING AND DECORATION
375g (12 oz) plain Marzipan (almond paste),
see page 26
peach, yellow, blue, red and green
food colouring
1 quantity Buttercream, see page 25
1 quantity Chocolate Moulding Icing,
see page 27
cornflour (cornstarch) for dusting
4 chocolate buttons
white chocolate chips (bits)
milk (German sweet) chocolate chips (bits)
1 liquorice 'bootlace'

● Preheat oven to 160°C (325°F/Gas 3). Grease two 1.1 litre (2 pt/5 cup) pudding basins and one 315ml (¹/₂ pt/1¹/₄ cup) pudding basin. Base line basins with circles of greaseproof paper (parchment), see page 9.
● Scrape cake mixture into basins and bake, allowing 35 minutes for small basin and 1 hour 10 minutes for large basins. Invert on wire racks to cool. Remove lining paper. Trim off top of cake baked in small basin to give rounded shape for clown's head.
● Melt plain (semisweet) chocolate and make chocolate case, following Steps 1–2 on pages 50–51. Colour half the marzipan (almond

paste) peach and two–thirds of the rest yellow. Colour some of remaining piece red and some blue, leaving a small piece plain. Shape two thirds of yellow marzipan into two flat boots. Position towards front of cake board.
● Reserve 3 tbsp of the buttercream for piping. Using remaining buttercream, assemble large cakes in chocolate case, following Step 3, page 51 and referring to Expert Advice on page 50.
● Cut off one third of chocolate moulding icing. Reserve a small piece of this, about the size of a plum. Divide the rest in half for arms. Roll into thick sausage shapes on surface dusted with cornflour (cornstarch) tapering each 'sausage' at end. Flatten slightly, then bend for arms. Neatly cut off thin ends for cuffs, referring to Step 4 photograph on page 50 for precise shape.
● Still keeping plum–sized piece of moulding icing aside, use the rest to cover clown body, following instructions in Step 4, page 50. Secure arms in position using a dampened paintbrush. Use a cocktail stick (toothpick) to mark elbow creases. Press chocolate buttons into front of clown to make shirt buttons. Dot shirt with white chocolate chips (bits).
● Roll a little of the peach marzipan (almond paste) into two balls for hands. Flatten slightly, then cut 4 slits for fingers, using a sharp knife. (See Step 5 photograph, page 51 for precise shape.) Attach clown's left hand to shirt cuff.
● Roll out remaining marzipan to a circle about 18cm (7 in) in diameter. Wrap around reserved small pudding cake, easing paste and smoothing ends underneath. Secure to cake to form clown's head. Pipe hair, following Step 5, page 51.

Continued on page 50

Continued from page 48

● Shape reserved chocolate moulding icing into a small hat. Decorate hat with a liquorice 'bootlace' band and a small flower made from red and blue marzipan (almond paste). Fix hat on top of clown's head.

● Make braces, following Step 6, opposite. Roll out remaining yellow marzipan (almond paste) and cut out a wide collar. Position around clown's neck and finish with a blue marzipan bow tie. Shape mouth and nose from red marzipan. For eyes use plain marzipan rounds, pressing a milk (German sweet) chocolate chip (bit) in the centre of each.

● Finally cut remaining liquorice 'bootlace' into short lengths; press into boots for laces.

EXPERT ADVICE

≈

When positioning second basin cake to make clown's body, place it towards back of chocolate bowl so that it almost touches the bowl, emphasizing the 'baggy trousers' effect around the front.

When chocolate moulding icing is placed over cake excess will fall in folds. Make sure this is at back of cake. Trim off excess icing with a sharp knife, then gently smooth down icing, using hands dusted with cornflour (cornstarch) to remove creases.

The easiest way to pipe buttercream 'hair' is to begin with a few guidelines to frame face area, then fill in and build up with plenty of piped lines.

~ 1 ~

Cover outside of a 1.4 litre (2½ pt/6¼ cup) pudding basin with foil, tucking ends neatly inside bowl and pressing creases as flat as possible. Melt chocolate and spread over foil to within 5mm (¼ in) of basin rim. Leave to set.

~ 4 ~

On a surface dusted with cornflour (cornstarch), roll out remaining chocolate moulding icing to a 25cm (10 in) round. Lay it over top cake, tucking ends inside chocolate bowl. Ease icing to fit around back of clown.

~ 2 ~

Carefully lift away foil tucked inside bowl. Twist bowl and remove it completely. With one hand gently resting in the base of the chocolate bowl, carefully peel away foil lining to leave a chocolate case.

~ 3 ~

Generously spread top of one large pudding basin cake with buttercream. Gently drop it into chocolate case. Position case on cake board, behind feet. Spread cake with buttercream; position second large cake.

~ 5 ~

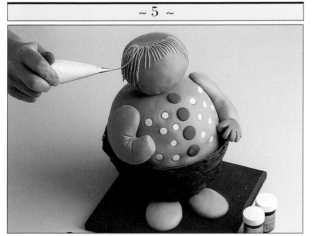

Colour reserved buttercream green and place in a paper piping bag fitted with a writing tube (tip). Starting from top of head pipe vertical lines of buttercream hair, short at front for fringe and longer around neck.

~ 6 ~

Roll out two strips of blue marzipan (almond paste), each about 28cm (11 in) long and 5mm (1/4 in) wide. Secure over clown's shoulders so ends just overhang trousers. Press chocolate chip (bit) into each end. Secure hand clutching brace.

MOCHA GATEAU

*T*his cake uses a Genoese cake base, but a Victoria Sandwich or Moist Rich Chocolate Cake could be used instead. The coffee flavouring added to both sponge and icing can be omitted if a plain chocolate gâteau is preferred.

4–egg mocha–flavoured Genoese Sponge
mixture, see page 11
155ml (¼ pt/⅔ cup) double (heavy) cream
1 tbsp icing (confectioners') sugar
¼ tsp vanilla essence (extract)
1 tbsp instant coffee powder
2 tsp boiling water
1 quantity Ganache, see page 28
DECORATION
60g (2 oz/ 2 squares) plain (semisweet)
chocolate
1m (1 yd 3 in) cream ribbon,
about 4cm (1½ in) wide
1m (1 yd 3 in) brown ribbon,
about 1.5cm (¾ in) wide

● Preheat oven to 180°C (350°F/Gas 4). Bake cake in two base–lined and greased 20cm (8 in) round cake tins (pans). Cool on a wire rack. Remove lining paper.

● In a bowl, whip cream to soft peaks, then continue whipping while gradually adding icing (confectioners') sugar and vanilla. Use to sandwich cakes together. Place on a flat serving plate.

● Dissolve coffee powder in measured boiling water in a cup. Make ganache mixture, adding the coffee after the cream. Leave until mixture is thickened but remains level in bowl.

● Pour ganache over cake and smooth down sides using a palette knife. Leave in a cool place to set.

● To make the chocolate lace motifs, make several tracings of the template on page 69 on the same piece of paper. You will need about 35 motifs, allowing for a few breakages. Secure tracings to a flat surface with a smooth piece of wax paper on top. Melt chocolate, put it a paper piping bag fitted with a writing tube (tip) and quickly pipe over lace motif outlines. Leave to set.

● Using an upturned bowl, cutter or pan, about 18cm (7 in) in diameter and with a very fine rim, carefully mark a central circle on top of cake. Decorate cake top with chocolate motifs, following instructions below. Chill until set.

● Just before serving, wrap ribbons around cake as illustrated opposite.

Carefully peel paper away from chocolate lace. Gently press motifs into marked circle, tilting each backwards and spacing them slightly apart.

EGGS IN A BASKET

*T*o achieve a true egg shape these chocolate eggs are moulded inside thoroughly cleaned egg shells before being dipped in melted chocolate. They are then arranged in a basket–shaped chocolate cake for a perfect Easter treat. If time is short, bought chocolate eggs could be wrapped in the same delicate ribbon and used instead.

---

12 large eggs
500g (1 lb/16 squares) plain
(semisweet) chocolate
500g (1 lb/16 squares) milk
(German sweet) chocolate
500g (1 lb/16 squares) white chocolate
Madeira Cake mixture, see page 12
double quantity chocolate–flavoured
Buttercream, see page 25
2m (2 yd 6 in) each of yellow, green and
burgundy ribbon, about 5mm (¹/₄ in) wide

● Start by making chocolate eggs. Using a clean skewer, carefully pierce a small hole in the thick end of one of the eggs. Break away a little of the shell to make a hole about 1cm (¹/₂ in) wide. Pierce yolk with skewer and pour contents out into a bowl. Repeat with remaining eggs.

● Thoroughly wash egg shells in warm soapy water. Rinse, then leave overnight on absorbent kitchen paper to drain, pierced ends down (see Expert Advice, page 56).

● Next day, arrange eggs in a clean egg box, pierced ends up. In separate bowls, melt 375g 12 oz/ 12 squares) each of the plain (semisweet) chocolate, the milk (German sweet) chocolate and the white chocolate. Fill the eggs with the melted chocolate, following the instructions in Step 1, page 56.

● Make cake. Preheat oven to 160°C (325°F/Gas 3). Following instructions on page 9, grease and base line a 3.4 litre (6 pt/15 cup) heatproof bowl with a circle of greaseproof paper (parchment). Spoon cake mixture into bowl and level surface. Bake for 1¹/₂–1³/₄ hours or until a skewer inserted into the centre comes out clean. Leave to cool in bowl.

● Remove cake from bowl and trim domed top level. Transfer to a cake board. Using a palette knife spread top and sides with about half the buttercream, smoothing down lightly.

● Place some of the remaining buttercream in a piping bag fitted with a writing tube (tip) and pipe basket, see Step 2, page 56.

● Remove chocolate–filled eggs from egg box. Roll them firmly on surface, then gently peel away shells to reveal chocolate eggs.

● Melt remaining chocolate in separate bowls. Roll a white chocolate egg in melted white chocolate. Lift out carefully between two forks, letting excess chocolate drip back into bowl. Place egg on a wire rack. Repeat with remaining eggs, dipping each in chocolate of the appropriate colour. Chill until set.

● Cut lengths of ribbon and use them to decorate the chocolate eggs, either tying them in bows or securing the ends with melted chocolate. Arrange eggs attractively in nest.

EXPERT ADVICE

≈

Don't be tempted to use a smaller bowl for baking the cake. The wide, shallow shape is essential if the basket is to look authentic.

EXPERT ADVICE

≈

Don't waste the real eggs. Use them in cakes or other dishes, but strain before use to remove any pieces of shell.

To make sure empty shells are thoroughly dry after cleaning, leave them overnight in the airing cupboard or in the oven once it has been turned off after cooking.

If removing the shells from the chocolate eggs proves difficult, place the eggs in the freezer for about 1 hour, then try again.

~ 1 ~

Spoon melted white chocolate into 4 shells, milk (German sweet) chocolate into 4 shells and plain (semisweet) chocolate into remaining shells. Leave in a cool place for several hours or overnight to harden.

~ 2 ~

Starting around top edge of cake, pipe short diagonal lengths of icing to create a rope work pattern. Pipe more rope bands under the first, working down to base of cake. Finish by piping a further rope band inside top rim.

Chequered Chocolate Parcel, see page 58

CHEQUERED CHOCOLATE PARCEL

Illustrated on previous page

*E*verything on this cake is edible, even the ribbon! Allow plenty of time for the decoration.

60g (2 oz/¹/₃ cup) plain (semisweet) chocolate chips (bits)
Madeira Cake mixture, see page 12
1 quantity Buttercream, see page 25
125g (4 oz/4 squares) plain (semisweet) chocolate
125g (4 oz/4 squares) white chocolate
¹/₂ quantity Modelling Chocolate made with plain (semisweet) chocolate, see page 20
¹/₂ quantity Modelling Chocolate made with white chocolate, see page 20
icing (confectioners') sugar for dusting

● Preheat oven to 160°C (325°F/Gas 3). Beat chocolate chips (bits) into cake mixture. Bake in a base–lined and greased 1 kg (2 lb) loaf tin (pan) for 1¹/₄–1¹/₂ hours until a skewer inserted into the centre comes out clean. Cool on a wire rack. Remove lining paper. Trim cake if necessary, see Expert Advice right. Cover with buttercream, following instructions in Step 1 opposite.

● Melt plain (semisweet) and white chocolate in separate bowls. Spread on separate sheets of wax paper as described on page 19. Leave to set. Use to create the chequered effect on the cake, following steps 2–3 opposite. Leftover chocolate squares can be used to make boxes, see page 19, if liked.

● Lightly knead both pieces of modelling chocolate. On a surface dusted with icing (confectioners') sugar, thinly roll each to a long strip. Using a sharp knife cut out thin strips from both colours, each about 5mm (¹/₄ in) wide. Lightly dampen edges of a white strip with a fine paintbrush dipped in water; sandwich between two dark strips to make a striped ribbon. Press strips together firmly. Use remaining modelling icing to make more chocolate ribbon in the same way.

● Measure the distance from centre of top of cake to base on each side. Cut four strips of striped chocolate ribbon of appropriate length. For bow, cut two 13cm (5 in) lengths of chocolate ribbon and pinch ends together to make loops. Cut two shorter lengths for ribbon ends, pinching one end of each together and cutting out a 'V' from opposite ends. Finally, secure chocolate ribbon to parcel, following Step 4 opposite.

EXPERT ADVICE

≈

The cake will probably 'dome' in the centre during baking. Slice top level once cake has cooled to create the parcel shape.

A square tin (pan) could be used for a parcel of a different shape. For a novelty parcel cover cake completely with plain (semisweet) chocolate and use fancy cutters to shape animal, star or crescent white chocolate cutouts for securing to cake.

Modelling chocolate will keep in a cool place for several weeks if tightly wrapped in a polythene bag. Break off pieces as required, kneading them lightly until pliable.

~ 1 ~

Using a palette knife completely cover cake with buttercream, making buttercream coating slightly thicker at top of sloping sides to give as square a shape as possible. Smooth down gently.

~ 2 ~

Cut out a panel from dark chocolate, exactly the same size as one long side of the cake. Cut the same in white. Repeat this process for remaining long side, both ends and top of cake. Cut all panels into even-sized squares.

~ 3 ~

Using appropriate panels for each cake side, peel off squares as required and secure to cake in chequered design, making sure squares line up neatly along edges. Continue design until cake is completely covered in chocolate squares.

~ 4 ~

Position the four prepared lengths of modelling chocolate ribbon so that they meet on top of the cake, brushing ends lightly with water to seal. Fix bow loops in position and add ends. Neaten centre of bow with a small piece of ribbon.

WOODCUTTER'S COTTAGE

*T*his chocolate variation on the familiar gingerbread house theme makes a good centrepiece for a birthday tea. Position three bears – made from modelling chocolate – at the front door to recall the story of Goldilocks. Although the cottage is hollow, it could be filled with a buttercream–covered rectangular chocolate cake to provide more servings.

315g (10 oz/2½ cups) plain (all–purpose) flour
60g (2 oz/ ½ cup) cocoa
(unsweetened cocoa powder)
½ tsp baking powder
185g (6 oz) butter, softened
185g (6 oz/1 cup) soft dark brown sugar
2 tbsp black treacle
(molasses or dark corn syrup)
2 eggs
DECORATION
250g (8 oz/8 squares) plain (semisweet) chocolate
125g (4 oz/4 squares) white chocolate
1 quantity chocolate–flavoured Buttercream, see page 25
30g (1 oz/1 square) milk (German sweet) chocolate
60g (2 oz) Chocolate Marzipan (almond paste), see page 26
4 large flaky chocolate bars (about ¾ cup shredded chocolate)
several chocolate buttons
icing (confectioners') sugar for dusting

● Make biscuit (cookie) dough. Sift flour, cocoa (unsweetened cocoa powder) and baking powder together. Beat butter and sugar together in a mixing bowl until just softened. Add treacle (molasses or dark corn syrup) and eggs with flour mixture. Mix to a soft dough. Knead lightly, wrap in greaseproof paper (parchment) and chill for about 30 minutes until firm.

● Trace cottage walls and roof on pages 69–71 on greaseproof paper (parchment). Cut out templates.

● Preheat oven to 190°C (375°F/Gas 5). Roll out some of the biscuit (cookie) dough on a lightly floured surface and lay it on a baking sheet. Cut out shapes, following Step 1 on page 63. Bake biscuit (cookie) shapes for about 10 minutes or until beginning to colour around edges. Leave on baking sheets for 5 minutes, then transfer to a wire rack to cool completely.

● Trace tree sections on page 68. You will need 5 tracings of large tree and 10 each of medium and small trees. On a separate piece of paper trace 12 window shutters and 1 door, using templates on page 69. Secure tracings to a flat surface with a smooth piece of wax paper on top. Melt plain (semisweet) chocolate and make runouts of trees, shutters and door, using technique on page 23. Leave to set.

● Melt white chocolate. Spoon a little of it onto the cottage walls. Spread with a palette knife, then make a swirled pattern over the chocolate with the tip of the knife. Repeat on remaining walls. Leave to set.

● Roughly spread a little of the buttercream over the surface of a 25cm (10 in) round cake board or flat plate.

Continued on page 62

Continued from page 60

● Assemble house. Generously spread inner ends of each wall with buttercream. Fix the four walls together, siting the cottage towards the back of the cake board or plate with the door facing the front. Position roof sections, following Step 2 opposite.

● Melt milk (German sweet) chocolate, put it in a piping bag fitted with a writing tube (tip) and pipe handles on the runout door and shutters. Shape a small chimney from chocolate marzipan (almond paste). Complete roof, following Step 3 opposite.

● Place 3 tbsp of the remaining buttercream in a paper piping bag fitted with a writing tube (tip). Spread the rest of the buttercream over the board around the cottage, piling it up in patches to create a 'hilly' effect.

● Peel shutters and door away from paper. Pipe a little of the buttercream on the back of each shutter runout and fix them in place. Finally add door, using buttercream as mortar, and fixing it slightly ajar.

● Shape trees and attach to cake board, following Step 4 opposite. Make a path from chocolate buttons. Finally, using a fine sieve, sprinkle cake and board generously with icing (confectioners') sugar.

EXPERT ADVICE

≈

For a tiled roof effect omit the flaky chocolate bars and use chocolate buttons instead. Chocolate runouts seldom break, but it is worth making a few extra tree and shutter runouts just in case!

TEMPERING COUVERTURE

❖

Couverture must be tempered before being used: Break up to 500g (1 lb) couverture into small pieces. Melt it in a heatproof bowl over a pan of simmering water. When chocolate reaches 46°C (115°F) on a sugar or chocolate thermometer, remove from the heat and place in a larger bowl of cold water. Stir chocolate until temperature falls to 27-28°C (80-82°F). Return bowl to heat and heat to 31°C (88°F). The chocolate is now tempered and ready for use.

~ 1 ~

Rest templates on biscuit (cookie) dough on baking sheet and cut around each, using a small sharp knife. Remember to remove windows. Lift away excess paste. You will need 2 roof shapes, 2 end walls and 1 of each long wall.

~ 2 ~

Generously spread the edges of one half of cottage roof with more buttercream. Gently rest one roof section in position so that point at top of walls is level with top of roof. Repeat on the other side.

~ 3 ~

Carefully spread roof with buttercream and position chimney. Cut flaky chocolate bars into 2.5cm (1 in) pieces. Cut each lengthways into 3–4 flat sections. Starting from bottom of roof, secure sections in position with chocolate overlapping.

~ 4 ~

Pipe several lines of buttercream up straight edge of one tree section. Holding this vertically, secure 4 more tree sections to the first, then transfer tree to buttercream-covered board. Make remaining trees in the same way.

WEDDING CAKE

*F*or the bride and groom who dislike traditional fruit cake but love chocolate, this has to be the ultimate wedding cake. Made entirely of chocolate and finished with chocolate leaves and flowers, it is also sure to delight the wedding guests! For colour contrast the flowers and leaves could be made using white chocolate or, for a dreamy winter wedding, the whole cake could be made in white chocolate and dusted with icing (confectioners') sugar.

15cm (6 in), 20cm (8 in) and 25cm (10 in) Moist Rich Chocolate Cakes, see page 14
triple quantity Apricot Glaze, see page 26
2.25kg (4½ lb) bought or homemade plain Marzipan, see page 26
icing (confectioners') sugar for dusting
4-egg white quantity Chocolate Moulding Icing (about 2.25kg/4½ lb) see page 27
cornflour (cornstarch) for dusting
250g (8 oz/8 squares) plain (semisweet) chocolate
18 modelling chocolate roses in various sizes, see page 20
36 chocolate leaves in various sizes, see page 24
ASSEMBLY
20cm (8 in), 25cm (10 in) and 30cm (12 in) round silver cake boards
6 lengths cake decorator's dowelling
6 clear cake pillars

● Place cakes on boards and brush generously with apricot glaze. Lightly knead 500g (1 lb) of the marzipan (almond paste). Roll out on a surface dusted with icing (confectioners') sugar to a round 10cm (4 in) wider than top tier. Lift over and fit around cake, using same method as for moulding icing, see Step 1, page 67. Trim off excess marzipan around base of cake. Cover remaining tiers in the same way, allowing 750g (1½ lb) marzipan for middle tier and 1kg (2 lb) for bottom tier.

● Weigh the chocolate moulding icing. Use about 500g (1 lb) to cover top tier, following instructions in Step 1, page 67. Trim off excess icing around base of cake. Cover remaining tiers in the same way, allowing about 750g (1½ lb) for middle tier and the remainder for the bottom tier. Reserve icing trimmings.

● Dampen edge of top tier cake board. Gather up icing trimmings and roll out thinly to a 2.5cm (1 in) strip. Use strip to cover exposed portion of board. Smooth down. Trim off any excess icing around edges. Repeat on remaining tiers. Leave overnight to harden.

● Mark position for dowelling on bottom two tiers of cake: Cut a 10cm (4 in) circle of greaseproof paper (parchment) and crease into thirds. Open out paper circle again and lay over centre of middle tier. Using a cocktail stick (toothpick), mark icing around edge of paper where each crease ends. Repeat this procedure on bottom tier, using a 13cm (5 in) circle of paper.

● Position dowelling and pillars in bottom and middle tiers, following instructions in Step 2, page 67.

Continued on page 66

Continued from page 64

● Cut out a 90 x 2.5cm (36 x 1 in) strip of greaseproof paper (parchment). Fold it in half three times so that when the paper is unfolded, it will be neatly marked in eight equal sections. Open out end section and lay it over template on page 68. Trace along dotted line. Re–fold template and cut along dotted line so that strip is scalloped when opened out. Use template to mark scallops around bottom tier, as described in Step 3 opposite, then repeat on remaining tiers.

● Melt plain (semisweet) chocolate. Put a little of it in a piping bag fitted with a writing tube (tip). Use to pipe decorations around cakes, following instructions in Step 3 opposite. Leave to set.

● Keeping best chocolate roses and leaves for top tier, arrange posies on centre of each cake as described in Step 4. Assemble tiers.

EXPERT ADVICE

≈

Make sponge cakes up to two weeks ahead and keep in an airtight container, or make several months in advance and freeze. Before decorating, drizzle cakes generously with brandy or an orange-flavoured liqueur. The marzipan (almond paste) and moulding icing can be applied a week ahead; it is not necessary to let marzipan harden before covering it with moulding icing.

Making large quantities of chocolate roses is time consuming, so make these several weeks ahead; store in a rigid container. Make leaves 2–3 days ahead.

If you prefer solid cake pillars to clear ones, trim dowelling level with tops of icing and sit pillars over ends.

~ 1 ~

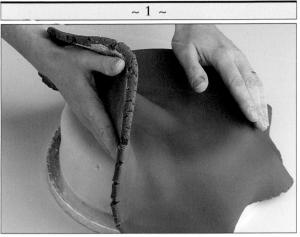

Roll out moulding icing on a surface dusted with cornflour (cornstarch) until 10cm (4 in) wider than diameter of cake. Lay icing over cake. Smooth icing down with hands dusted with cornflour, easing excess to fit around sides.

~ 2 ~

Press three dowelling lengths vertically down to base of cake through marked positions. Set pillars over dowelling. Mark position where dowelling reaches top of pillars. Remove pillars, saw off dowelling ends; replace pillars.

~ 3 ~

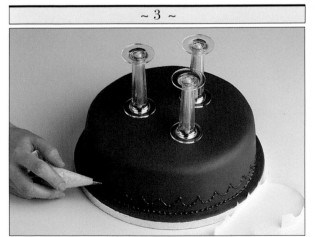

Using a pin, fasten paper template around bottom tier, with straight edge against base. Use a second pin to prick out outline of scallops on cake. Pipe a 'snailtrail' around cake base and over scalloped line, see page 22.

~ 4 ~

Using a little melted chocolate in a paper piping bag, secure roses attractively around pillars, pressing down gently into position. Arrange leaves around roses, propping them against roses and pillars.

TEMPLATES

Wedding Cake, page 64

Fluted cake edge

Woodcutter's Cottage, page 60

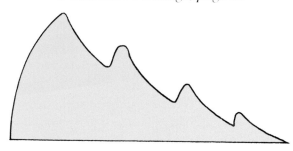

Small tree, make 10

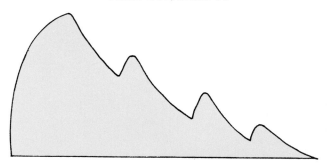

Medium tree, make 10

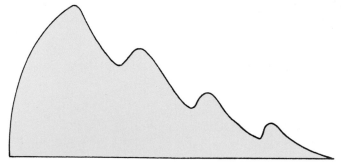

Large tree, make 5

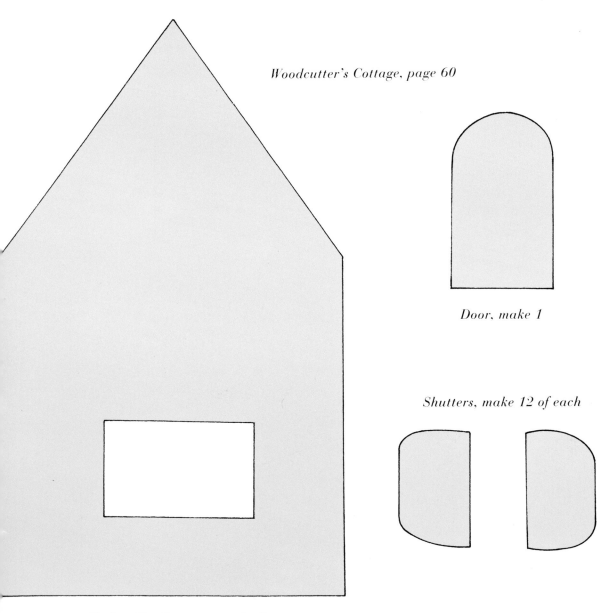

Woodcutter's Cottage, page 60

Door, make 1

Shutters, make 12 of each

End walls of cottage, make 2

Mocha Gateau, page 52

Lace motifs

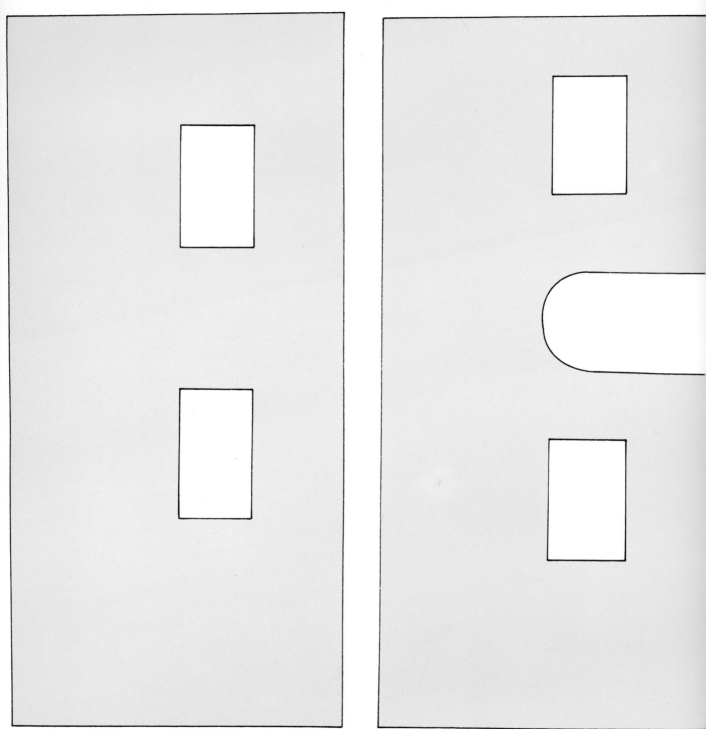

Cottage back wall, make 1

Cottage front wall, make 1

Cottage roof, make 2

INDEX

FOR FURTHER INFORMATION

Merehurst is the leading publisher of cake decorating books and has an excellent range of books to suit cake decorators of all levels.
Please send for a free catalogue, stating the title of this book:–

United Kingdom
Marketing Department
Merehurst Ltd.
Ferry House
51–57 Lacy Road
London SW15 1PR
Tel: 081 780 1177
Fax: 081 780 1714

U.S.A/Canada
Foxwood International Ltd.
P.O. Box 267
145 Queen Street S.
Mississauga, Ontario
L5M 2BS Canada
Tel: (1) 416 567 4800
Fax: (1) 416 567 4681

Australia
J.B. Fairfax Ltd.
80 McLachlan Avenue
Rushcutters Bay
NSW 2011
Tel: (61) 2 361 6366
Fax: (61) 2 360 6262

Other Territories
For further information
contact:
International Sales
Department at United
Kingdom address.